THE 5 PRINCIPLES OF
IT CUSTOMER SERVICE SUCCESS

THE 5 PRINCIPLES OF
IT CUSTOMER SERVICE SUCCESS

A COMPASSIONATE GEEK®
GUIDE FOR IT PROFESSIONALS

DON R. CRAWLEY
CSP™, LINUX+, IPv6 SILVER ENGINEER

This book identifies and uses product names and services known to be trademarks, registered trademarks, or service marks of their respective holders. Such marks are used throughout this book in an editorial fashion only. Additionally, terms suspected of being trademarks, registered trademarks, or service marks have been appropriately capitalized, although Crawley International Inc. cannot attest to the accuracy of such information. Use of a term in this book should not be regarded as affecting the validity of any trademark, registered trademark, or service mark. Neither the author nor Crawley International, Inc. is associated with any vendor or product mentioned in this book.

For information about special discounts for bulk purchases, contact Crawley International Inc., PO Box 48094, Seattle, WA 98148-0094.

Telephone: (206) 988-5858
Email: don@doncrawley.com
Website: http://www.doncrawley.com/

Reasonable attempts have been made to ensure the accuracy of the information contained in this publication as of the date on which it was written. This publication is distributed in the hope that it will be helpful, but there are no guarantees made as to the accuracy, reliability, or applicability of this information for any task or purpose whatsoever.

The author recommends that these techniques be used only as a guide to working with end users and customers. Under no circumstances should these techniques be considered universal rules for working with all people in all situations.

C'Est Bon Press
Seattle, Washington
United States of America

ISBN: 0-9836607-7-8
ISBN-13: 978-0-9836607-7-4
Library of Congress Control Number: 2016911770

DEDICATION

This book is dedicated to the millions of talented and hardworking IT people in the world, without whom we would not have the data networks that make possible worldwide sharing of knowledge. This worldwide collaboration has resulted in a global awakening the likes of which the world has not experienced since the Renaissance. If the world survives, it will be thanks, in large part, to the geeks and nerds.

In memory of Michael J. Costello.

CONTENTS

x

PREFACE

This is *perhaps* my fourth IT customer service book. I say perhaps because I've been writing about IT customer service for about ten years in the form of workbooks, blogs, and books. This book, unlike my earlier books, attempts to deal only with point of view. It is not about scripts and protocols for dealing with IT customers. Instead, it focuses exclusively on how we see ourselves within an organization and within the context of human interactions.

I heard a speech by R. Robert Cueni in which he seemed to speak directly to me. After his talk, I asked him, only half joking, how he managed to direct his comments to me specifically. He replied that he writes speeches for himself and hopes that the lessons are relevant for others, too. So it is with my books. This book is written about my process of self-discovery, transformation, and growth. I hope the lessons I'm learning on this journey are as relevant and useful to you as they have been to me.

I developed the 5 Principles of IT Customer Service Success over a period of about ten years as I traveled through the United States, Canada, and other countries working with IT staff on both customer service skills and technical skills. I observed that there are two broad groups of IT people. In the first group are people who are enjoying interesting and satisfying careers and lives. In the second group are people whose careers and lives leave them bored and dissatisfied. The former are positive, upbeat, and a joy to be around. The latter are cynical, negative, and soul-draining. As I taught and worked with various groups of people, I began to wonder whether certain identifiable traits were associated with people in the first group that would be valuable for me to share with my students. As I continued my work with IT people, I saw five traits begin to emerge among people in the first group. These provided the foundation for the 5 Principles of IT Customer Service Success.

I've created boxed text at various points throughout the book to highlight key points and ideas for you to consider.

ACKNOWLEDGMENTS

Thanks, as usual, to Janet, my wife. Thanks, also, to Paul Senness and Sandy Brown who probably don't even realize how they model compassionate living for everyone around them.

CHAPTER 1:
AN INTRODUCTION
TO SERVICE

People in the IT world ask whether technical skills or customer service skills are more important for someone working in IT. That's the wrong question. The right question is whether technical skills or *people* skills are more important. Not everyone who works in IT is involved in customer-facing jobs, but most of us are involved in jobs that require varying levels of human contact—and thus people skills. Even tenured coders must occasionally use people skills to persuade others of their ideas, to negotiate terms of employment, or to navigate an interpersonal issue with another human, perhaps a coworker or a boss.

Still, that doesn't tell us which is more important.

Harvard social psychologist Amy Cuddy suggests that when someone meets you for the first time, that person quickly answers two questions about you:

Can I trust this person?

Can I respect this person? (Cuddy 2015)

These two questions allow us to assess warmth and competence. Warmth is related to your people skills, and competence is related to your technical ability. The most successful people tend to have both.

My son, Jon, worked as an inside technical recruiter at Google. He observed that job candidates' technical skills would get them interviewed, but their collaborative skills would get them hired. The same phenomenon has been described by Dr. Daniel Goleman in his work on emotional intelligence. Goleman noticed that a person's IQ (intelligence quotient, or raw cognitive ability) would get him or her a job, but that person's EIQ (emotional intelligence quotient, or people skills) was the best predictor of long-term career success. (Goleman 1995)

Another way of looking at this is through the competence/charisma four-quadrant model.

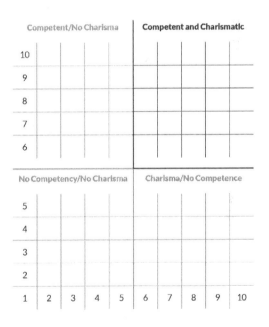

Figure 1. The Competence/Charisma Four-Quadrant Model

In this model are four quadrants related to technical skills (competence) and people skills (charisma). For the purpose of this discussion, we will define competence as your ability to perform the core aspects of your job. If you are a surgeon, for example, your competence is your ability to perform surgical procedures. If you are an accountant, it is your ability to understand and implement tax laws, to abide by the Generally Accepted Accounting Principles, and to balance books. If you are a server administrator, it is your ability to successfully design, configure, and manage a Linux file server or a Windows Domain Controller. For the purpose of this discussion, we will define charisma as your ability to understand, get along with, and influence people.

In the lower left quadrant are people who have neither competence nor charisma. These are people who have given up on themselves as well as on society. They don't pursue knowledge, they blame everyone else for their problems, and, in the worst cases, they exhibit extreme antisocial behavior, such as murder-suicides or terrorist acts. You certainly don't want to be in the lower left quadrant!

In the lower right quadrant are people who have no technical skills but who are good at dealing with other people. They are skilled at manipulating people, but they bring nothing of substance to the relationship. In extreme cases, these are con artists. You don't want to be in the lower right quadrant, either!

In the upper left quadrant are people who are competent but who lack charisma. They have technical skills—sometimes extremely well-developed technical skills—but they have trouble getting along well with others. The fictional character Dr. Sheldon Cooper from the television series *The Big Bang Theory* comes to mind.

We also see this sometimes with professional athletes. An athlete might perform exceptionally well on the gridiron or a basketball court but get in trouble with the police for antisocial behavior when the game is over. In the workplace, you might see a highly skilled computer programmer who is very good at coding but who lacks people skills. When I worked as a radio station program director, we had a chief engineer who was very talented and knowledgeable about electronics, but he was brusque and rude and had poor personal hygiene. He was so good at electronics that we tolerated his antisocial characteristics for a while. Ultimately, however, he became so difficult to work with that we replaced him with another highly competent engineer who was much easier to work with. The problem with people in the upper left quadrant is that they frequently have an unrealistic and inflated view of how good they are at their jobs. They overestimate their value to the organization or to other people. When it is time for layoffs or furloughs, their names are often at the top of the list. They might be surprised when the organization terminates their employment. They might blame the organization and its managers for incompetence and then go through the same experience with their next employer. Similarly, they might blame other people for not including them in social activities when the real reason why they are excluded is because they are so difficult and unpleasant to be around. There are very few people who are so technically skilled that people and organizations will tolerate bad interpersonal behavior over the long term.

A joke often told by professional speakers describes how a speaker asked his spouse how many truly great speakers were in the world. The reply? "One fewer than you think." Be careful not to overestimate your value to an organization and not to underestimate the importance of people skills to your career success. Genuine humility and a sense of service to others are traits of many successful people.

In the upper right quadrant are people who have both competence and charisma. These are the leaders in our society. Several names may come to your mind, but I will mention three: Bill Gates, Mary Barra, and Elon Musk. (It is purely coincidental that two of the three are involved in the automotive industry.) These people combine high levels of technical competence with the ability to understand, get along with, and influence people. It is important to note that likeability is not necessarily part of this equation, although there are certainly times when it can be helpful. Characteristics of people in the upper right quadrant include a strong work ethic, an unquenchable thirst for knowledge and enlightenment, curiosity, and an understanding of the psychology of human relationships. The three people mentioned as examples of successful leaders are well known, but fame is not one of the requirements for making it into the upper right quadrant. You probably know individuals who are both technically gifted and who have an ability to understand, get along with, and influence other people.

Here's how to use the model in your own life and career: Consider where you are at this moment in terms of both your competence (technical skills) and your charisma (people skills). It really doesn't matter where you place yourself. What matters is that you honestly assess your personal strengths and weaknesses and then make a personal commitment to do something every day to move toward the upper right corner in the upper right quadrant. You might want to ask for input on your strengths and weaknesses from a mentor or similar person who is successful and whom you respect.

(Many of us are our own worst judges!) Your goal is to strive every day to be as good as possible with both your technical skills, or competence, and your people skills, or charisma.

You may be asking yourself which is more important—technical competence or people skills. Both are critically important. An accurate and thorough job description really answers the question. Having said that, however, in a technical job, your technical skills must come first. Without deep technical skills, you simply can't do your job. How deep depends on the job. We certainly wouldn't want an aircraft mechanic who was great with people but who was technically incompetent working on our airplane right before a flight. Nor would we want a neurosurgeon who had a great bedside manner but who had lousy surgical skills operating on our brain. That suggests that your technical skills are the most important skills to have. Remember, however, the Google principle of interviewing based on technical skills but hiring based on collaborative skills. Also, recall Daniel Goleman's ideas about IQ being the minimum cognitive ability (brainpower) required to do the job but EIQ being a better predictor of long-term career success. Again, the job description will define the level of technical competence required. Additionally, some organizations may hire based on a candidate's having a minimum acceptable level of technical competence with the idea that he or she can be trained on the job to a higher level of technical competence.

Some managers say they hire people based on their customer service skills because technical skills can be taught on the job, or vice versa. Although I've heard managers say that you can't teach people skills, this is simply wrong. The key is whether an individual is willing to invest the time and effort required to master people skills. Frankly, the same thing applies to technical skills.

An unwilling student is unlikely to learn. A willing and committed student can and will learn the needed skills for success.

INTRODUCING THE 5 PRINCIPLES OF IT CUSTOMER SERVICE SUCCESS

Let's begin by defining *principle*. A principle is a fundamental basis of something—in this case, IT customer service. It is also defined as a fundamental truth. The fundamental truth of customer service, IT or otherwise, is that it involves service to others: it is caring about your brothers and sisters, your fellow human beings.

In my previous books, I have described the four traits of customer service masters. Those four traits revolved around people skills; I took technical competence for granted. But as I have continued my work with people in technical positions, I realized that I was wrong to make that assumption. Thus I will speak of five traits, or principles, including technical competence.

The 5 Principles of IT Customer Service Success map to the competence/charisma model. The first, as I've mentioned, is the hard skill principle of deep technical competence, which obviously maps to the competence component of the model. The second through fifth are the soft skill principles of compassion, empathy, listening skills, and respect, which map to the charisma component.

Deep Technical Competence

From the customer's perspective, our deep technical competence is measured by our abilities to troubleshoot problems quickly, solve them permanently, and design systems that work seamlessly with minimal interaction.

Compassion

Compassion is combining a profound awareness of another's suffering with a desire to alleviate it. Compassion is noticing people who are hurting—then trying to help them.

Empathy

Empathy is the ability to put yourself in another's shoes, feeling what another is feeling. If you have ever wanted to jump through the phone and strangle a customer service representative for not understanding what you were going through, you have encountered a lack of empathy. On the other hand, if you have ever felt that a customer service representative really understood you, your problem, and your frustration, then you were encountering empathy.

Listening Skills

The ability to listen—*truly* listen—to our sisters and brothers is one of the greatest gifts we can give each other. When we focus on the other person and what he or she is saying instead of focusing on ourselves and what we want to say in response, we are telling the other person that he or she is important. We are saying that the other person's words, thoughts, and feelings matter.

Respect

Respect has two aspects. One is when we feel respect for another person because of his or her words and deeds. The other is when we treat people with respect and dignity. In the former instance, people must earn our respect. It is about how we feel about them; it is internal to us. In the latter instance, it is about our behavior toward other people. It is external to us. We need not feel respect for someone to treat him or her with dignity and respect.

THE 5 PRINCIPLES OF IT CUSTOMER SERVICE SUCCESS

HARD SKILLS	Deep technical competence
SOFT SKILLS	Compassion
	Empathy
	Listening skills
	Respect

In the following chapters, you will learn how the 5 Principles of IT Customer Service Success can shape your career, your relationships (both personal and professional), and even your life.

You can watch a video of my keynote address at which includes the 5 Principles at this link: http://www.doncrawley.com/KeynoteVideo.

CHAPTER 2: THE PRINCIPLE OF COMPETENCE

N ow let's explore the 5 Principles of IT Customer Service
Success, the first of which is deep technical competence.

WHAT DEFINES DEEP TECHNICAL COMPETENCE?

Deep technical competence will be defined differently based on
the job requirements, the organization, and the environment.
The technical competence level required of a desktop support
technician, for example, will be considerably different from
that required of a database administrator working for a large
ecommerce site or of someone developing encryption algorithms.
Similarly, the technical competence requirements of someone
working for a large enterprise organization will be different from
those of someone working in a small business. This is not meant
to suggest that one competence level is greater or more important
than the other. It could be—or it could just be a different set
of skills. Certainly the technical competence requirements for
someone who is responsible to protect nuclear missile launch
codes will differ from the requirements of someone whose job is
maintaining a retail point-of-sale system. All jobs are important.

It is not a matter of valuing one type of job, organization, or environment over another but simply a matter of different situations' requiring different competencies at different levels.

HOW MUCH TECHNICAL COMPETENCE IS REQUIRED?

This question has a two-part answer. Certainly you must have deep enough technical competence to fulfill your job description. (Obviously, that will vary from one job to another.)

> *It is a good idea to occasionally review your job description to ensure that you are maintaining sufficient technical competence to meet (or exceed) the requirements of the description.*

THE NECESSARY LEVEL OF TECHNICAL COMPETENCE ALSO DEPENDS ON THE INDIVIDUAL

But also consider yourself, your career goals, and your personal commitment to excellence. Suppose that your job description requires that you have a technical competence level of (say) 60. It's an arbitrary number, but think of it as the minimum level of technical expertise required to do your job. Some people will be satisfied to perform at a level of 60, but they won't be able to solve more complex and interesting problems. They won't receive merit-based pay increases or promotions—and, frankly, they probably won't win much respect from their peers. They may even feel as if they know more than they actually do and might occasionally (although perhaps unintentionally) provide inaccurate information to customers, clients, colleagues, and end users. If you are satisfied with a minimum skill level similar to what I just described, you should be aware that your job is at risk thanks to automation and outsourcing.

Some other people might see 60 as the minimum skill level required for their job and then strive for higher levels of performance. Their natural curiosity leads them to use the minimum skill level as a launching point for learning as much about their work and the products they support as possible. Perhaps they strive for a technical competence level of 70. These individuals are more likely to get promotions and merit pay increases and to gain the respect of their peers.

Still others might strive for a technical competence level of 80. These individuals not only work to improve their technical competence but also are curious about the overall workings of the business. They are interested not only in IT systems but also in accounting, marketing, production, and all the various other systems and departments that contribute to the performance of the organization.

Still others may strive for a competence level of 90 or even higher. These individuals not only strive for excellence in technical competence but also branch out beyond their particular areas of specialization into all aspects of IT. They work to understand how the business works overall, and they are insatiably curious about how the world works. They are voracious readers, and their hobbies and interests stimulate them mentally. They are curious about other people, and they spend more time asking questions than making statements when in conversation.

The more valuable you make yourself, the more secure you will be in your job and career. This point is becoming more and more relevant as we see the growth of automation, including robotics, and outsourcing. The people whose jobs will be most secure in the future are those who strive to make themselves as valuable as possible to employers and customers.

OUR ACTIONS REVEAL THE TRUTH OF OUR DESIRES

A *New York Times* reader once commented, "We seem to get the life we want, whether or not we realize we want it." Our actions reveal the truth about our desires. Those of us who focus our efforts, our time, and our lives on becoming the best we can be in every pursuit, whether technical, moral, academic, or otherwise, demonstrate what we really want in life. Oddly, even if we don't feel compelled to achieve excellence, the act of pursuing excellence can reframe our innermost wants and desires and transform our lives. As we think, so we act—and, paradoxically, as we act, so we think. American football coach Vince Lombardi once said, "We are going to relentlessly chase perfection, knowing full well we will not catch it, because nothing is perfect. But we are going to relentlessly chase it, because in the process we will catch excellence."

A good way to think about this is that you must have sufficient technical competence to solve technical problems quickly and permanently. In addition, your technical competence must be deep enough to allow you to anticipate and prevent future problems. You gain this deep level of skill through education, reading, experimenting, and experience. Attend seminars, workshops, and conferences. Go back to school to take courses related to your field. Work on professional level certifications such as those offered through CompTIA, Microsoft, Cisco, LPI, and other organizations. Set up test labs at home or in the office using virtualization tools such as VMWare, HyperV, or VirtualBox. Strive to be the best in the world at the technologies you support.

I once attended a day-long workshop on the Linux boot process to learn more about Linux-based operating systems. Although I learned a great deal about how Linux boots, I also learned about other operating systems. The instructor commented that the more you know about one operating system, the more you know about them all. In my experience, the more knowledge you have, the better you understand all things.

Many IT people, especially in the early stages of their careers, will build complex data networks in their homes for the purpose of experimenting and gaining practical, hands-on experience. I once had a client who wanted me to develop a workshop on VoIP (Voice Over Internet Protocol). Although I had a good understanding of VoIP, I didn't have much hands-on experience with it. I decided to build an Asterisk server for my home and deployed extensions for my wife, each of my children, and myself. (The kids didn't care for it at all, but they rolled their eyes and tolerated it!) The experience I gained in the process was invaluable in developing the training program for my client.

In the same way, even if you don't become the best in the world, the act of striving for that type of performance will make you exceptionally excellent.

WHAT SHOULD YOU TAKE AWAY
FROM THIS CHAPTER?

At the end of each of the five chapters in which I introduce the
5 Principles of IT Customer Service Success, I will provide one
takeaway. Consider it an action item for you to work on.

Takeaway #1

Take personal responsibility to strive to be the best in the world
at whatever it is you do. Your company and colleagues might not
support you in your endeavor, but this is not about them. It's about
you. Regardless of whether you become the best in the world, in
striving toward that goal, you will achieve excellence.

CHAPTER 3: THE PRINCIPLE OF COMPASSION

The second principle is compassion, the act of caring about the well-being of another.

In customer service, there are two distinct approaches to compassion. The first approach involves teaching people compassionate-sounding words and phrases to use when dealing with customers. Though well meant, this approach can make customer service providers sound stilted and phony. Even so, it is a widely used approach in customer service training. You've probably experienced a customer service or technical support representative saying memorized or scripted words such as, "Mr. Crawley, I'm sorry you are having a problem with our product, and I will get it taken care of for you." But there's no feeling behind the words—they are merely being recited verbatim, because the representative has been trained to use those exact words and phrases. But when words have no feeling behind them, they ring hollow. Customers can perceive the difference, even if they don't say anything about it.

It is understandable why companies might choose to use a scripted approach to customer service. Scripting provides consistency of support. Additionally, if a company's front-line support staff members must work with people from a different culture than their own, scripting provides a means of overcoming cultural differences. Although I understand why some companies choose a scripted approach to customer service, it is not a way to build positive relationships with customers, and it can be off-putting when executed poorly.

The second approach involves helping people develop an innate sense of compassion. When you are able to truly feel compassion, you don't need to be told the words to say or the actions to take. They come naturally.

Being compassionate means combining a profound awareness of another's suffering with a desire to alleviate it. When our end users and customers place themselves in our care, they are first of all human beings—our brothers and sisters. We might not like their political views, and we might not like how they look or act. Even if we don't like anything about them, they are still human beings deserving of our care, understanding, and respect. When you genuinely care about what happens to other people—when you are truly compassionate—you instinctively look for ways to better their experience.

There is a large body of anecdotal evidence to suggest that living a life filled with positive emotions can have a positive physiological effect on our bodies. Like most people, I enjoy hearing stories that reinforce my preconceived notions about the world. I also recognize that anecdotes are often great stories, but they are not scientific, and they can often lead to poor decision-making.

Perhaps like you, I've heard stories about how living a more compassionate and empathic life can improve our health, so I thought I'd see whether there's any research to back up the stories. I found that in 1997, the journal *Integrative Psychological and Behavioral Science* conducted a study of forty-five healthy adults. The adults in the experimental group experienced significant increases in positive emotions and significant decreases in negative emotions. Additionally, the experimental group experienced a 23 percent reduction in cortisol levels and a 100 percent increase in levels of the hormone DHEA. According to research conducted by the National Institutes of Health, DHEA is possibly effective for, among other things, countering the effects of aging on skin and bones. Cortisol is often cited as the "stress hormone," for it is released during periods of high stress to help us deal with stressful situations. When present in the body for long durations, however, cortisol is associated with several negative effects, including impaired cognitive performance, decreased bone density, decrease in muscle tissue, higher blood pressure, and lowered immunity. It seems clear, then, that living a life filled with positive emotions, including compassion and empathy, can have powerful positive effects on our bodies and our minds. The question, then, is how we can become a more compassionate and empathic person. Here are five practices that can help you become even more compassionate and empathic than you already are.

EXPRESS GRATITUDE

Start by expressing gratitude. We've all been blessed in our lives. Certainly some people might seem to have been blessed more than others, but each of us has gifts for which we can be grateful. A gift might be something big and complex, such as a college education, or it might be something as simple as a beautiful day. Think of those things; reflect on them—focus on them.

LOOK FOR COMMONALITY INSTEAD OF DIFFERENCES

Practice thinking of what you have in common with others. As different as we all are, we are also quite similar. In a June 2007 article in The Optimist magazine (formerly *Ode Magazine*), writer Tijn Touber suggests an exercise. When you meet someone or even just see someone on the street, discreetly go through a reflection similar to this:

- *Like me, this person seeks happiness.*

- *Like me, this person wants to avoid suffering.*

- *Like me, this person has a history that includes suffering, loneliness, despair, and sadness.*

- *Like me, this person wants to fulfill his or her needs.*

- *Like me, this person is still learning about life.*

None of us has it all figured out.

LOOK FOR WAYS TO HELP

Look for ways to relieve suffering. They don't have to be anything big, although they might be. You might do something as simple as feeding a stranger's parking meter, picking up a piece of trash, holding the door for another person, or paying the toll of the driver behind you.

PRACTICE BEING KIND

Practice being kind, especially to people whom you don't like or trust. It is easy to be kind to your friends and to people whom you trust. It is a much greater challenge to be kind to people whom you find disagreeable. To really put yourself to the test, practice being kind, compassionate, and respectful, even (or especially) to people who mistreat you.

SLOW DOWN

Finally, slow down. I've noticed that I'm the least compassionate when I'm in the greatest hurry.

In a well-known experiment conducted at Princeton Theological Seminary (Batson, 1973) (Darley and Batson, 1973), several students were told to go to a different building to deliver a speech that was to be recorded. Half the students were assigned to give a talk on the Christian parable of the Good Samaritan, a story about compassion. The other half were given a different topic. The students were given different deadlines for completing the assignment. The students came from different moral and religious backgrounds. On the path to the second building, the students encountered an actor portraying a victim, slumped in a doorway, needing assistance. The objective of the study was to identify the conditions under which a student would stop to render aid.

The students who were in the greatest hurry were the least likely to stop and help.

The lesson seems obvious: slow down. To the best of your ability, slow down to allow yourself to become more compassionate.

Make compassion a daily practice. When you wake up in the morning, think of what you can do that day to be kinder and more caring—not only to your fellow humans but also to animals and the world around you. At the end of each day, pause and reflect on what you did during the day to be kinder and more compassionate. In short, *be intentional about being kind and compassionate.*

Of course, compassion is only one part of the formula for being great at serving others—but it is a great start. Not only will having a sense of compassion help us as we strive to improve our customer service, but it will also help make us better humans!

> *The best way to show compassion for customers is to handle their issues quickly, accurately, and efficiently in a positive, respectful, and professional manner.*

Takeaway #2

Being compassionate means that when others are hurting, you notice—and you try to help.

CHAPTER 4:
THE PRINCIPLE OF EMPATHY

The third principle is empathy—the ability to connect with another individual emotionally, to feel what he or she is feeling. It is often known as "putting yourself in someone else's shoes." In my customer service workshops, I recommend the use of empathetic phrases such as "I'd feel that way, too, if it happened to me" or "I can hear how frustrated you are, and I don't blame you." However, as with compassion, scripted or memorized words and phrases can seem hollow when they don't come from the heart. For that reason, it is important to be authentic in your empathy. If you simply can't relate to the other person's situation, it is okay to say so when you combine it with honest human understanding. For example, you can say things like "I've never been in your situation, so I'm not going to tell you I understand. I can't even imagine what that's like, but I am going to do everything possible to help you." Be careful though; if you are simply saying the words without trying to understand what the other person is going through, you'll come across as phony or condescending. Your objective is to show sincere human-to-human empathy.

> *Paradoxically, the overuse of scripted empathetic words
> and phrases can convey a lack of empathy. Think about
> a time, for example, when you might have been trying
> to take care of an issue with a company and you just
> wanted to get the issue resolved. Unfortunately, the
> customer service rep might have kept reciting scripted
> and insincere (but well meant) empathetic words and
> phrases over and over, thus delaying the resolution of
> the problem! Offer a quick word of empathy and then
> take care of the issue.*

Empathy is the ability to put yourself in the other person's position, to feel and understand what he or she is are experiencing. Empathy, combined with technical competence, is a powerful formula for success at work.

Here are some ways to be more empathetic.

IMAGINE HOW YOU WOULD FEEL

Think about how your user or customer must feel when she or he is preparing a last-minute report for a boss and the printer dies. Imagine how an executive feels when he or she is getting ready to give an important presentation to a group of high-level execs and the computer locks up or the projector fails. Imagine the frustration of a researcher who has been collaborating with another researcher by working remotely—and then the Internet goes down. Imagine how you would feel if the same thing were to happen to you. Recall how you felt the last time you were working on a project, perhaps editing a long router configuration file, and your computer bluescreened.

LISTEN

Being a good listener shows compassion and helps establish empathy. When we truly listen to other people, we learn their story. Listen with the intent of understanding the speaker. Stop your mental chatter, put down your smartphone, and really listen to the other person. To make this work, when we listen, we must focus our attention entirely on the other person and avoid the temptation to mentally prepare our response, to interrupt, or be dismissive. (We'll talk more about this shortly—listening is also the fourth principle.)

ALLOW HUMAN-TO-HUMAN CONNECTION

Dr. Edward Hallowell coined the term human moment to describe a time when two people connect with each other. (Hallowell, 1999) According to Hallowell, technology has made it possible to do business without human contact. Yet it is through human contact that we develop human connections, which are a necessary ingredient of healthy living. If you are working in an IT department in which all customer contact is via telephone, chat, or email, find a way to connect in person with other people, even if they are not your customers. In Hallowell's human moment, you turn off the iPad, close the book, and give your full attention to the other person, and you do it in person.

USE EMPATHETIC LANGUAGE

Using phrases such as "I'm sorry that happened to you," "I don't blame you for feeling that way," or "I'm sure I'd feel the same if I were in your position" can help us reflect on the other person's experience. Of course, the words and phrases themselves don't do the trick. You must be sincere in saying them, but the act of saying empathetic words and phrases can serve to make us more aware of what our sisters and brothers are experiencing. Sincerely expressed empathy can also help to defuse emotionally charged situations.

Be very careful about saying phrases such as "I know how you feel." Even if you've had similar experiences to the person with whom you are speaking, you can't know exactly how he or she is feeling. Even saying "I know how you feel" has the potential to devalue what the other person is saying and feeling. It makes the conversation more about you than the other person. Conversations with customers must be more about the customer than about you. Empathetic language can be very powerful. Used incorrectly, it can be powerfully bad.

DON'T BE JUDGMENTAL

As one human to another, it is not our job to be judgmental. Yes, we all do it, but within the context of a customer support interaction, being judgmental can create barriers to support. Understand that we all approach life from a unique perspective— that no one's experience is the same as another's. Sure, most of us are judgmental at times. In fact, being judgmental is part of our evolution. It allows us to escape threatening situations when we judge them to be dangerous. Still, our twenty-first-century world has become polarized and filled with judgments: *If you disagree with me, you are obviously wrong and not worthy of my time.* That sort of judgmental behavior can undermine relationships and even careers. Remember the words of author Tom Kida: "Don't believe everything you think." (Kida 2006)

PRACTICE CURIOSITY ABOUT OTHERS

Part of being empathetic is being interested in other people. Ask questions about where they are from, their work, and their background. Let them talk without jumping in with your own perspective. You can't learn about other people while talking about yourself. Don't force this type of conversation. Remember that your customer's time is valuable and that his or her primary goal is to quickly resolve whatever the problem is. It's also important to remember that your company's time is valuable. In addition to respecting your customer's time, you must also remember to respect your employer's time.

CHALLENGE YOUR OWN PREJUDICES

Just because you believe something doesn't mean that it is true or that it is the only truth. Author Tom Kida, as mentioned previously, says it very well in the title of his book *Don't Believe Everything You Think*. Put yourself in situations in which you might hear philosophical or political discussions that differ from your beliefs and just listen. Seek to gain an understanding of the opinions of people whose beliefs are diametrically opposed to your own.

Recall Stephen Covey's fifth habit from the *Seven Habits of Highly Effective People*: "Seek first to understand, then to be understood." (Covey, 1989, 2004)

LOOK FOR COMMONALITIES

As with compassion, look for commonalities instead of differences. Yes, each of us is unique, and we have many differences among us—but we also have a lot in common. You can't learn what you share with other people when you focus on your differences.

I have a good friend who believes that the Earth is 6,000 years old. I believe that it is about 4.5 billion years old. If I focused on his belief about the age of the Earth, I would miss the opportunities we enjoy to spend time together pursuing our shared interests.

LOSE THE LABELS

Avoid labeling people. It is a lot easier to hate a label than a person. When we get to know each other as people, not as liberals or conservatives; Democrats or Republicans; Christians, Jews, or Muslims; blacks or whites; men or women; or any other labels, we realize that in spite of our differences, we are all connected in many ways.

Being empathetic with customers builds trust, helps build stronger relationships, and reminds us that people are not machines; they have feelings.

Building empathy has all kinds of benefits. There are many studies showing that children who are taught empathy are less aggressive, have lower levels of stress and depression, and do better academically. (To learn more, search the Internet for "benefits of teaching children empathy.")

Empathy is a foundation for morality. In the presence of empathy, it is difficult for cruelty to exist (Baren-Cohen 2011). Empathy heads off some conflicts before they start, prevents other conflicts from escalating, and is a key component in conflict resolution. If we are going to be masters at customer service, whether in IT or in any other field, our ability to empathize with our fellow humans is key to success in today's workplace.

> *As with compassion, the best way to show empathy for customers is to handle their issues quickly and efficiently in a positive, respectful, and professional manner.*

Takeaway #3

Having empathy means that you try to understand and feel what others are feeling. Being empathetic means that you can relate to their frustration and anger even if you don't agree with their reasons for being frustrated or angry.

CHAPTER 5:
THE PRINCIPLE OF LISTENING

The fourth principle is the ability to listen, meaning that your sole focus is on what the other person is saying. Being a great listener takes practice, so don't expect to master this skill the first time you try it. Effective listening means focusing on the other person instead of on yourself. Many of us listen attentively—and, while listening, prepare our response. To be a great listener, focus entirely on understanding what the other person is saying. Recalling Stephen Covey's wisdom in *The Seven Habits of Highly Effective People* (Covey [1989] 2004): Listen with the intent to understand, not just respond. A technique that can help is to listen as though you are going to be tested on what is being said. If you know there's a quiz, you'll find a way to sharpen your focus on the speaker!

We listen at five different and distinct levels. How you listen to your end users and customers will significantly affect your success and that of the overall IT support team—and, for that matter, your entire organization. As important as how you actually listen is how you are perceived as listening.

Here are the five levels of listening.

IGNORING

The lowest level of listening is called ignoring—not listening at all. If you are distracted by anything while talking to users, they can get the impression that you are ignoring them. For example, suppose that while the user is speaking, you start a conversation with a colleague at work. You are ignoring your user. In your personal life, you may have experienced a time when you were trying to talk with someone who was Facebooking or engaged with his or her smartphone. You were in the same room with the other person, but you might as well have been a thousand miles away. That person was ignoring you. It didn't feel good, and that's exactly how our customers feel when we do other activities while they're trying to talk with us.

PRETEND LISTENING

Pretend listening is most easily explained in the face-to-face conversation when a person makes sounds as though he or she is listening but actually is not. On the phone it happens when you say things like "I see" and "okay" while working on an unrelated email, checking social media, or playing a computer game. People can tell when you are distracted.

SELECTIVE LISTENING

During selective listening, we pay attention to the speaker as long as he or she is talking about things we like or agree with. If the speaker moves on to other things, we slip down to pretend listening or ignore them altogether.

> *For years, I spoke of how teenagers were masters at the art of selective listening. Then it dawned on me where my teenagers had learned that skill. They had learned it from me! At that point, I began to work on changing my own listening behavior.*

ATTENTIVE LISTENING

Attentive listening occurs when we carefully listen to the other person, and while he or she is speaking, we decide whether we agree or disagree, determining whether the speaker is right or wrong while preparing our response.

At all four of these levels, it should be evident that we are listening to our own perspective—in most cases, intending to respond from our experience. Our focus is on ourselves, not the speaker.

EMPATHIC LISTENING

Empathic listening, also known as empathetic listening, is the highest level of listening. To be successful in providing IT support to end users, you must teach yourself to treat every call as though it is the first time you have ever heard of such a problem, even though you may have heard similar ones many times before. Discipline yourself to see it through the eyes of the user. Similarly, when a colleague is explaining a problem or an issue, you must listen closely, aiming to understand what he or she is saying. Empathic listening is the highest level of listening, and it is the hardest to accomplish.

To achieve empathic listening, slow down, be patient, talk less and listen more, ask questions when you do talk, and paraphrase what was said to ensure you that didn't overlook anything.

At the end of the call or visit, briefly recap what you have discussed, what approach you are suggesting, and any follow-up needed on your part or the customer's part. Be specific about how you will follow up, what you will do, what the customer can expect, and when it will happen.

A great way to evaluate whether you are doing empathic listening is to ask yourself *Where is my focus?* Is your focus on the other person, or is it on yourself?

As you think about the five levels of listening, consider that the first four levels are self-focused, whereas the fifth level (empathic listening) is focused on the user. When your focus is completely on the user and not on yourself, your level of service will be much higher.

Because many of us love lists, here is a top-ten list of ways to be a better listener:

10. Lose distractions.

9. Don't finish thoughts or sentences for the other person.

8. Don't get defensive.

7. Paraphrase what you just heard.

6. Listen to understand, not just respond.

5. Make good eye contact.

4. Allow natural pauses in the conversation.

3. Ask relevant and open-ended questions.

2. Keep an open mind.

1. Stop talking!

Being a good listener is one of the great gifts we can give to our brothers and sisters. When we listen—truly listen—to another person, we are saying that the other person is important to us and that we value what he or she says and thinks, even if we don't agree with it.

Takeaway #4

Being a good listener means focusing on what the other person is saying, not on what you want to say in response. You strive to understand the meaning of what is being said regardless of whether you agree with it.

CHAPTER 6:
THE PRINCIPLE OF RESPECT

The fifth principle is treating all people with respect, regardless of how we might feel about them. In fact, it is not necessary to respect someone to treat him or her with respect. Respecting someone is a matter of how you feel about that person and whether he or she has earned your respect. It is internal to you. Treating someone with respect, however, is external. It is about your behavior—and, frankly, is often a reflection of how you feel about yourself. People who have a high level of self-respect tend to treat everything around them more respectfully.

In our roles as providers of service to people, we can find ourselves dealing with people we don't like or respect. We maintain our own dignity and self-respect when we treat all living things respectfully. In Viktor Frankl's landmark book *Man's Search for Meaning*, he says that the true measure of an individual lies in his or her ability to maintain a sense of dignity in all circumstances (Frankl [1946, 1959, 1962] 1984). In short, even when we are treated disrespectfully by others, we must rise above the fray and act in a respectful and dignified manner. We are setting an example for others through our actions and behavior.

Sometimes doing this might seem difficult, especially when you don't like or respect the other person or when you feel that person has disrespected you in some way. But the act of treating someone with dignity and respect is about you and your behavior, not about the other person.

> *It is not necessary to respect someone to treat her or him with dignity and respect.*

EIGHT WAYS TO SHOW RESPECT FOR OTHERS

Be Punctual

If you say you are going to be somewhere at 2:00, then be there at 2:00. If you find yourself frequently saying things like "Sorry I'm late, the traffic was awful" or "Sorry I'm late, there was a train blocking traffic"—or "Sorry I'm late" followed by any other excuse—you need to leave earlier. We are not late because of traffic. We are late because we didn't leave early enough. Even more than that, Bernard Roth, in his book *The Achievement Habit: Stop Wishing, Start Doing, and Take Command of Your Life* (Roth 2015), points out that the real reason we're late to a meeting, for example, is because we did not consider that meeting important enough for us to be on time. If it is important enough, you'll leave early enough.

Consider this: If you have an opportunity to meet one of your heroes, but you must be at a certain location at exactly 10:00 a.m. or you'll lose the opportunity to meet him or her, you'll be there on time. No excuses!

I used to be perpetually late for almost everything. Then my boss at the time pointed out that it was rude and inconsiderate. I know it seems obvious, but I hadn't thought of it in those terms before. After that I began focusing on being punctual.

Put simply, being late is rude and disrespectful. It says that your time is more important than everyone else and that it is okay for other people to wait for you.

Lose the excuses, and start leaving earlier. My sons had a football coach who told his players, "If you are not fifteen minutes early, you are late!" That is good advice.

Compliment the Achievements of Others

It is important to be sincere in this. We're all better than we used to be at spotting phonies. If you are not really impressed by what the other person did, you can certainly be excited that he or she is excited. It's called *positive empathy*, and it's about another person's positive emotions. Here's an example: My wife, Janet, doesn't care a thing about computers or networks, but when I come running upstairs excited because I got an IPSEC VPN tunnel to work between two disparate devices, she gets excited for me. She doesn't give a rip about IPSEC VPNs, but she cares about me, so she shares in my excitement. Your customers and end users are important to you, too. Share in their excitement.

The 5 Principles of IT Customer Service Success

Be Sincere and Authentic

As I just mentioned, we're pretty good at spotting phonies. Avoid using a lot of the typical business clichés. You can certainly say things like "It is good to see you" or "I'm glad to help," but you should avoid automatic apologies. If you find yourself automatically saying "I apologize" to your customers, especially over and over, that is a sign that you are falling into cliché and insincerity.

Do What You Say You'll Do

It is really pretty simple. Just do what you say you'll do. If you are not going to be able to do it—whatever *it* is—don't say that you will.

If you commit to doing something and circumstances beyond your control prevent you from completing it, proactively get in touch with everyone who will be affected by the change to let him or her know about it. Deliver the news as quickly as possible.

Lose Sarcasm

Sarcasm is off-putting. It is condescending, and there's really no place for it in human relationships. Sure, it's fine if you are a standup comedian—but otherwise, don't do it.

Be Polite

Say "please" and "thank you." Follow the rules for being a good listener. Be gracious in your dealings with your fellow humans. Remember—this applies to everyone. One of the ways to measure a person is in how he or she treats people who have nothing to offer.

Respect Other People's Time

Much as with being punctual, this is about not wasting other people's time.

When you are speaking with other people, be aware of their schedules and time constraints. We all know people who talk on and on. Perhaps they are under the mistaken impression that they are fascinating conversationalists, but they are not. Being a good conversationalist is about listening as much as, or more than, you are talking. Perhaps these people are nervous and talking on and on is just nervous chatter. Regardless, remember that people have schedules, obligations, and work to get done. Though some light conversation is often okay, be careful about letting it go on too long, and watch for signs that the other person wants to get going.

Don't Make Fun of Other People

Some people feel that it is okay to laugh at other people and make fun of them. I wonder how they would feel if the tables were turned.

We all make mistakes, we all have struggles, and we all have our quirks and unique combinations of personality traits. When we make fun of other people, what we are really saying is *You're different from me. I'm right and you are wrong, so you need to change to be more like me.* That seems awfully presumptuous. Don't make fun of other people, and don't make jokes about other people, either to their face or behind their back. Instead, try to understand them, even if you don't agree with them.

Making fun of other people, joking about other people, and name-calling are all signs of small-mindedness.

EACH OF US REPRESENTS ALL OF US

In 2015, I had the honor of working with a group of IT staff members in the Sultanate of Oman. One of the people in my group pulled me aside during a break to tell me that Omanis are taught at an early age that each one of them represents the entire population of Oman. Think about it. If you meet only one person from Seattle, that person's behavior is a reflection on the entire population of Seattle. It's not fair at all, but it is often true that we form an opinion based on a single experience. If we IT people are rude, disrespectful, or condescending, we run the risk that others will form an opinion of all IT people as being rude, disrespectful, and condescending. However, if we are polite, helpful, and respectful, we go a long way toward helping people see all IT personnel as being polite, helpful, and respectful.

Each one of us represents all of us.

Takeaway #5

You need not respect someone to treat him or her with respect. The act of respecting someone is internal to you; it is how you feel about the other person. The act of treating someone with respect is external—it is about your behavior. It is also a reflection of your character and how you feel about yourself.

CHAPTER 7: IMPLEMENTING THE 5 PRINCIPLES

Of course, it is not enough to just read about the 5 Principles of IT Customer Service Success—you also must implement them in your life.

The process of implementing these principles starts when you make a personal commitment to incorporate them in your everyday life. It sounds easy—and it *should* be easy—but it can be hard to do by yourself.

Accordingly, work with a partner so that you'll have accountability. I was amazed at how much more writing I got done when I agreed with a partner to commit to an hour of writing each day. She and I check in with each other once each week to see how we are doing, and I really don't want to let her down.

Keep a log. Get a loose-leaf binder or a spiral notebook. At the beginning of each day, write down what you'll do that day to live out each of the 5 Principles of IT Customer Service Success. Here are some examples:

- *Technical competence:* Today I will read a chapter and watch a video on how to build Cisco router access lists.

- *Compassion:* Today I will be kind to that person who was grumpy yesterday.

- *Empathy:* Today I will ask the administrative assistant in the finance department to help me understand the hardest part of her job.

- *Listening:* Today, while the finance department's administrative assistant is talking with me, I will avoid sharing my ideas. Instead, I will ask questions and work to ensure that understand what he is explaining to me.

- *Respect:* Today I will maintain my own sense of dignity and respect while treating everyone and everything around me with dignity and respect. I will refrain from joking about others.

Make the log personal. The ideas I mentioned above are just ideas—thought-starters for you. It is important that you make a commitment to work on real issues you deal with, either at work or in your personal life.

At the end of the day, go back to your goals, and write down what you did to accomplish them. There may be times when you don't accomplish all of your goals. Talk with your partner about what happened and why you didn't reach them. Don't make excuses. If the goals are important enough to you, you'll find a way to accomplish them—if not the first time, then on subsequent tries.

Here are some examples of what your log might look like:

MORNING GOAL SETTING

- *Technical competence:* Today I will build my technical

  competence by: _____

  _____

- *Compassion:* Today I will become more compassionate by:

  _____

  _____

- *Empathy:* Today I will become more empathetic by:

  _____

  _____

- *Listening:* Today I will become a better listener by:

  _____

  _____

- *Respect:* Today I will show more respect for others by:

  _____

  _____

EVENING ACCOUNTABILITY

- *Technical competence:* Today I improved my technical

   competence by: _____

   _____

- *Compassion:* Today I showed more compassion for someone

   by: _____

   _____

- *Empathy:* Today I showed more empathy for someone by:

   _____

   _____

- *Listening:* Today I was a better listener to someone by:

   _____

   _____

- *Respect:* Today I showed more respect for someone by:

   _____

   _____

How long should you do the daily exercise of setting the goals and keeping the log? In 1960, Dr. Malcolm Maltz published the best-selling book *Psycho-Cybernetics*, in which he shared his observation that it takes a *minimum* of about 21 days to change mental images. Although that has become a popular number, it was based on informal observations, not on scientific data. The authors of a 2009 study found that creating new habits took anywhere from 18 to 254 days (Lally 2010). In short, there is no "magic number," even though it is certainly appealing to think of such things. Rather, prioritize the areas in which you want to grow, make a personal commitment to that growth, find a partner to hold you accountable, and start working on yourself!

Realize that, just as with spirituality, music, art, philosophy, sport, or any other worthwhile endeavor, personal growth is a lifelong process. There is no destination; there's only the journey of continual self-improvement.

There is no magic formula, no magic pill, and no magic number. You've simply got to do the work.

CHAPTER 8:
LIVING THE 5 PRINCIPLES

Living the 5 Principles of IT Customer Service Success means making a personal commitment to three I's of living: integrity, interest, and intentionality.

A LIFE OF INTEGRITY

Living a life of integrity means committing to honesty. In his book *Lying*, author Sam Harris mentions numerous times when it would be perfectly understandable to be dishonest, yet in each of those cases, the dishonest person must then live with his or her dishonesty (Harris 2013). People who have integrity do what they say they are going to do. You can count on them. People who have integrity don't have to spend the rest of their lives living with the knowledge that they let someone down.

Living a life of integrity means agreeing to do only what you know you will be able to do. It means learning how to say no gracefully.

A LIFE OF INTEREST

Living a life of interest means committing to curiosity about other people and the world in which we live. The most interesting people I've known are the people who are most interested in other people and in the world. Be a person of questions more than a person of statements.

Cultivate an unquenchable thirst for knowledge. Turn off your television. Read. Read ideas that contradict your most deeply seated beliefs. Attend lectures. Listen to thoughtful, educated people on all sides of issues. Seek to achieve an empathetic understanding of those who feel and believe differently from you. It is not necessary, nor even desirable, for you to agree with them. It is important, however, for you to grasp how and why they feel and believe the way they do.

People who live a life of interest stop to look up words they don't know, check the location of countries they don't know, and don't get defensive when others challenge them. You will never hear a person who lives a life of interest say that he or she is bored. Such people are curious about everything.

A LIFE OF INTENTIONALITY

Living a life of intentionality means having a purpose for the things you do in your life. Some people drift with the wind, accepting what life hands them. Other people are intentional in their lives. They set goals and work toward them. They give real thought to the choices they make—including the potential consequences of their actions.

Being intentional means taking full responsibility for yourself, your actions, and your life. Certainly there are some situations that are beyond your control. In *Man's Search for Meaning*, Viktor Frankl reflects on his experiences in Nazi concentration camps and describes freedom as a condition of the mind and liberty as a condition of the environment. (Frankl [1946, 1959, 1962] 1984). Nelson Mandela, during the twenty-seven years of his imprisonment, did not have liberty of movement, but he did have freedom of thought. Similarly, you might not be able to control your job, colleagues, workplace, customers, or other aspects of your environment. You can, however, control how you view them and how you respond to them.

CHAPTER 9:
SHARING THE 5 PRINCIPLES

How can you share the five principles of technical competence, compassion, empathy, listening, and respect?

Model these five principles at work, at home, and with your friends. Changing the behavior of others is difficult (sometimes it is nearly impossible), and if it is going to happen, it will start when we change our own behavior as a model for how we want others to behave.

I talked to a corporate group recently about compassionate customer service. After the talk, one of the managers asked me how he could get his staff members to show more compassion and caring for their customers. I told him that it begins with him modeling the behavior that he wants from his staff. People don't do as we say—they do as we do.

Talk with the leaders you know—perhaps teachers, clergy, managers, and civic leaders—about these five principles. The principles are simple and easy to remember. It is not difficult to create disciples who will help spread the word to others.

Consider teaching these five principles to others. If you can teach a subject in a way that others understand it, you must know it well. So it is with these five principles.

Can you share these five principles with your family, friends, and colleagues in such a way that they understand and embrace them?

The following are some other ways in which you can share these principles and, in the process, master them yourself. Form a book club based on this book. Get a group of friends together for the purpose of reading and discussion. Read a chapter each week (or each month, or at whatever interval works for your group) and then discuss it. You'll find a book group leader's discussion guide available for download at www.doncrawley.com/bookgroup.

Form a Meetup group (www.meetup.com). You can start with an hour-long weekly meetup on customer service following the 5 Principles of IT Customer Service Success. After covering all five principles, work on other areas of customer service. Alternatively, use this book as a launching pad for discussions on compassion, empathy, listening skills, and respectful behavior.

SEVEN ESSAYS ON
IT CUSTOMER SERVICE

ESSAY 1: HOW TO HANDLE COMPLAINTS IN 3 PRACTICAL PHASES

Watch the companion video at https://youtu.be/DEN6lPuDVq4

Customer and end user complaints are a fact of life if you work at the help desk. They are not limited, however, to the help desk. All of us in IT at one time or another have to deal with complaints. Perhaps the complaints are from an end user or a customer, or maybe they are from a colleague, a vendor, or your boss. Regardless of who is complaining, our ability to handle complaints effectively with grace and aplomb is a mark of our people skills and our emotional intelligence.

You can use the acronym LOF to remember the three phases of handling complaints.

L is for Listen

During the listening phase, we use our best listening skills. We listen respectfully without finishing thoughts or sentences for the other person, we allow the person to vent, we ask open-ended questions to gather information, we empathize, and we sincerely apologize. We are careful not to become defensive. We assume that the person who is complaining has a valid point. (If it turns out later that the complaint was not a valid one, we can deal with that then. During the initial phase, let's assume that the person who is complaining is right.) After listening, we paraphrase what we heard to ensure that we understand the complaint correctly.

O is for Offer a Solution

After listening and coming to agreement about the nature of the complaint, we offer a solution. Sometimes crafting a complete solution may require time and thought. In that case, we say so and offer a time frame for presenting the complete solution. But if we are able to craft a complete solution on the spot, we offer it and come to agreement with the other person.

F is for Follow Up

The final phase of handling complaints—and, in my experience, an often overlooked phase—is to follow up to confirm that the solution is working. Perhaps you follow up later that day, the next day, or several days later. That will depend on the nature of the complaint and the solution. Regardless, you must follow up to ensure that the complaint has been resolved and that the solution is working. A quick phone call or email is all it takes. Try saying something like "I'm following up on your complaint about the network printing problem. How is everything working now?"

Many people think of handling complaints as a difficult chore. There certainly are times when it is very challenging and not at all fun. However, many complaints can be handled pleasantly and effectively using the mnemonic LOF: listen, offer a solution, and follow up.

ESSAY 2: HOW TO DEAL WITH AN IRATE CUSTOMER OR END USER

Watch the companion video at https://youtu.be/Ux_wXxU_meI

Most people are reasonable most of the time. Occasionally, however, even reasonable people have meltdowns. Sometimes, unfortunately, we may also have to deal with someone who is a jerk. Regardless, it is not easy to deal with an irate customer or end user and still provide good customer service. After a recent speech, an audience member approached me and asked whether she is just supposed to "take it" when people are really angry. That's a tough question, because our ability to manage even the most difficult human-relations problems is one of the measures of our success at providing good customer service. It does seem a bit unreasonable to expect support desk or other IT staff members to tolerate the ranting and raving of someone who is very upset. Still, even though it may be unreasonable, our career success may depend on our ability to successfully navigate encounters with people who are very upset.

Assume the Other Person Is Right

Start by assuming that the other person is right to be really angry. Later, if it turns out that the other person was wrong, you can discuss things in a less emotionally charged atmosphere. But by assuming that the other person is right, you can display sincere empathy for him or her, from one human to another. In the presence of sincere, human-to-human empathy, even a very angry person will often start to regain his or her composure.

Don't Put Yourself in Danger

Hopefully, you'll never have to deal with someone who scares or threatens you. In that unlikely event, you must protect yourself by going to a safe place immediately. If someone is threatening you on the telephone, transfer that person to your supervisor right away. (Before you make the transfer, let your supervisor know what happened so that he or she isn't blindsided.) Different people have different thresholds for verbal abuse. Think ahead of time about how far you are willing to let someone go. Talk with your supervisor ahead of time to discuss expectations.

Pause and Breathe

In my lessons on emotional intelligence, I talk about the importance of pausing for a moment when dealing with emotionally charged situations. When you encounter someone who is very angry, pause for just a moment to manage your own emotions before you react. Take a deep breath (or two or three) and then work to maintain your calm. When we respond immediately in anger, we run the risk of saying something we will later regret.

Listen Carefully and Be Patient

Give the person the gift of being a good listener. Perhaps he or she needs to vent and you happen to be the person who answers the phone or who shows up at his or her cubicle at the moment when he or she reaches the boiling point. Listen for meaning without judging the other person or thinking of your response.

It Is Not Personal

In most cases, the customer's rant is not personally directed at you, so don't take it personally. If the customer does start to make personal insults, you can try saying something like, "I'm here to help you, and I want to help. I understand that you're angry and frustrated. It will be easier for me to help you if you don't insult me."

Empathy Is Powerful

Offer sincere human-to-human empathy and sympathy for the customer's problem. Use your own words to say something like "I'm so sorry that happened" or "Wow, I don't blame you for being upset—I'd feel the same if that happened to me." Make sure you are authentic in what you choose to say. Otherwise, you run the risk of being perceived as a condescending phony or someone who is just reading from a script. That will only make things worse.

Speak Softly

It is an odd paradox that our words are more powerful when spoken softly than when spoken in a loud voice. (Obviously, though, from a practical standpoint, you must ensure that the other person can hear you.)

Janet, my wife, was an award-winning middle school teacher. She noticed that, when the kids in her classroom were noisy and rowdy, the best tactic was for her to stand at the front of the room and speak in a normal tone of voice. Eventually, the students would quiet down. Conversely, if she yelled at them, the room only got louder. There is power in restraint.

Headline and Own the Problem

Headlining means that you say what you are going to do. Owning the problem means that you take personal responsibility for resolving the issue. Perhaps you might say something like this: "I can get you a temporary laptop right now. I will make sure it has the software you need and connect it to your cloud storage so you'll have all your files. Then I will walk your existing laptop through troubleshooting and let you know what we find, along with the next steps." Obviously, you must consider company policy before you promise. Don't make promises that you can't keep.

Take a Few Minutes for Yourself

Dealing with angry people is tiring. Once you've gotten the situation under control, take five minutes and go for a walk around your building, watch a funny YouTube video, take a few long, deep breaths, or splash cool water on your face.

Dealing with angry people is never fun—it is draining. But it is also sometimes a part of our job in IT. The ability to handle even an angry or an irate customer with respect and dignity is a mark of an emotionally intelligent individual and can contribute to long-term career success.

For additional insights, see my blog post on dealing effectively with angry Type A customers at http://www.doncrawley.com/how-to-deal-with-an-angry-type-a-customer/.

ESSAY 3: THE IMPORTANCE OF THE BUSINESS MINDSET IN IT CAREERS

Watch the companion video at https://youtu.be/QVU5Cy-ECtM

I frequently receive calls and emails from potential clients who say something like this: "Our IT staff is filled with highly intelligent, very talented individuals who are great at solving technical problems, but they don't understand that we are a business." Then they talk about how great the IT staff is with the technical aspects of their job—but how they are difficult to work with, don't understand that they work for a business, and don't realize that they have to deal effectively with people in order to do their jobs.

Here's the cold reality: In business, unless you are contributing to profitability, your job is always at risk. If you work for a business, you must always be making a positive contribution to the profitability of the business. If you work for a nonprofit or a government entity, you must always be making a positive contribution to the mission of the organization. When standing in line at the registrar's office at the university I attended, waiting to pay my tuition and fees, I overheard one of the staff members say, "This job would be great if it were not for the darned students." I sometimes encounter IT staff members who say something similar. They complain about end user requests and odd behaviors. Many of their complaints are perfectly understandable, and yet, were it not for end users, we wouldn't have jobs. We must always remember that our jobs are not just technical in nature. Our jobs are about crafting creative technical solutions to perplexing human problems in the workplace. Our jobs are about providing caring and compassionate service to our coworkers, who are trying to do their jobs.

This means that we work to create an open and inviting atmosphere in our public-facing areas. If we have tech cafes, kiosks, or similar support options, they need to be bright and inviting places for nontechnical people to visit. We need to immediately acknowledge our end users and customers when they come to visit. We need to always be friendly professionals and create an atmosphere in our end user–facing areas that speaks of friendly professionalism. Even if we don't have public-facing areas, we must still strive to be seen as friendly professionals.

Many end users are intimidated by IT people. That needs to change. Many managers are frustrated by IT staff who seem aloof and arrogant. That also needs to change. Certainly many of us are well-meaning, but we can unintentionally come across as arrogant and aloof. Regardless, it is important for all of us who work in IT to also work on our people skills, understanding that our departments exist solely to support the business and the people— our colleagues—who work in it.

ESSAY 4: THE PROBLEM WITH OVERSHARING WITH CUSTOMERS (TMI)

Watch the companion video at https://youtu.be/ek0hhqh3NT4

I called customer service at a large company. The phone was answered by a friendly woman who seemed helpful. While she was waiting for some information to appear on her screen, she started making small talk. Then it happened. She started talking about her recent medical procedures. That is bad enough—and, to make things worse, she went into great detail. TMI (too much information)! I had been on the phone with her for about 30 to 40 seconds, and I didn't know her at all, yet she was disclosing deeply personal information that would have been appropriate to share only with her physician or close family members. It certainly was not appropriate information for her to share with a customer over the telephone! Why? Oversharing of intimate personal details, including ailments, aches, and pains, is off-putting and can make a customer uncomfortable or worse—and, frankly, most people simply don't want to hear it. Nothing good will come of oversharing, and it can even drive customers and end users away.

When Janet and I were on a walk recently, we exchanged pleasantries with a woman who was sitting on a park bench. Shortly after our conversation started, however, she began giving us her medical history. We couldn't wait to move on. Similarly, one of our friends has multiple medical conditions. Far from simply giving us a quick update and moving on to something more positive and upbeat, they are all she talks about.

Or consider what happened when a family member was accidentally cut with a sharp knife. We went to urgent care for treatment, and the person handling intake started talking about how drunk he had been recently and how sick he had been. He didn't know us at all, yet he was disclosing his irresponsible behavior to us, undermining our trust in his competence. In addition, it was in very poor taste! Again—TMI.

Crossing the Line in Sharing Personal Information

I'm not sure what the fascination is with medical conditions or why some people wish to share such details with strangers, but it certainly happens far too often for my preference. I don't know where the line is between sharing appropriately with friends and oversharing, but I do know that sharing such information with customers and end users is rarely appropriate.

Be a Friendly Professional in IT Customer Service

In my keynote talks and seminars, I often speak of the need to be a friendly professional. That means that we conduct ourselves in a personable manner while taking care of business. In particular, we should follow the rules for polite conversation: Avoid religion, sex, and politics—and medical conditions.

There are certainly times when it is desirable to make small talk, such as while waiting for information to appear on a screen or for a computer to reboot. Use that time to talk about sports, the weather, kids or grandkids, pets, work, travel, hobbies, or where you are from (home town, neighborhood, or country). Ask questions of the other person. Keep things positive and upbeat. Find something to compliment about the customer or his or her company or city—or anything else. By the same token, avoid complaining—and, by all means, avoid oversharing or giving TMI in customer service!

ESSAY 5: HOW TO ANSWER THE PHONE IN IT CUSTOMER SERVICE

Watch the companion video at https://youtu.be/h9t6kzXj2Ic

This seems so simple and so obvious, yet I continue hearing people answer the telephone the wrong way. It is just like your parents said: you have only one chance to make a good first impression. The manner in which you answer phone calls is what creates that first impression. Do it correctly and the call will go better. Do it wrong and you'll lose credibility, you'll fail to make a human-to-human connection with your caller, and your call won't go nearly as well.

Sometimes people answer the telephone in a brusquely or gruffly: "Tech support." Sometimes they sound bored. Other times they answer with a lengthy script in which they recite their technical certifications and even beg for evaluation scores by stating their evaluation objective. Sometimes they sound so syrupy sweet that they come across as condescending. To see all three improper phone-answering techniques in action, visit my YouTube channel at https://youtu.be/h9t6kzXj2Ic.

The correct way to answer the telephone is with a greeting that is simple, upbeat, professional, and short: "Technical support. This is Don. How may I help you?"

But what if your company requires you to recite a long, ridiculous script? First, show your supervisor my video on how to answer the phone. If that doesn't work, do your best to understand the motivation behind requiring the script, and then practice it with a friend and work to make it as believable as possible. Good luck!

ESSAY 6: WHAT TO DO IF YOUR COMPANY WON'T PROVIDE TRAINING

> Watch the companion video at https://youtu.be/pmwMdjQ24iw

A well-trained workforce is one of the best ways to ensure a company's success. It seems like common knowledge, yet often companies provide inadequate training or even no training at all. What should you do if you work for such an organization?

Some people might choose to coast, doing as little as possible. They might say to themselves *The company doesn't care, so why should I?* It is certainly understandable that they would feel that way. The problem, however, is that not only does the company suffer from such an attitude, but the same attitude also affects the person who feels that way—and it affects that person's customers, his or her fellow humans. I once flew on an airline that was having labor problems. The members of in-flight staff were rude to the customers even though the customers had nothing to do with the labor problems. It was as though the in-flight crew members were so angry at the airline that they wanted to do everything possible to create a bad experience for everyone else. They forgot that, from one human to another, we are all deserving of each other's care and compassion.

What Are Your Training Options?

Another approach you can take if your company doesn't provide the needed training is to take the responsibility to make yourself as good as possible in spite of your company's actions (or inaction). Perhaps your company doesn't provide customer service training despite the proven value of good customer service. There are many books on customer service (like this one), there are videos, there are blogs, and there are many other sources of training on customer service. If you want to have a successful career and life, take personal responsibility for making yourself as good as possible at your job even if your company doesn't seem to care. It is a matter of having personal pride in your work and caring for your fellow human beings, your sisters and brothers who come to you for help.

Technical Training and Certifications

The same thing applies to technical training and certifications. When I'm conducting training, I frequently ask whether the participants are working on technical certifications. Often they answer that because their company doesn't offer any incentive to achieve certifications, they don't care, either. I point out that certifications can be a matter of pride and can help improve one's chances in future job searches—and that the certification preparation process can help fill in knowledge gaps.

The more knowledge you have, the easier your job becomes. You'll gain self-respect along with the respect of your friends and colleagues. Knowledge is power, especially when it is self-motivated.

Additionally, as artificial intelligence gets better and better and the use of robotics continues to grow in the workplace, it just makes sense to make yourself as valuable as possible to help ensure your job security.

Do you want to get a better job, a raise, or a promotion? Do you want to stay employed in a rapidly changing world? Take personal responsibility for making yourself as valuable as possible. Invest in yourself regardless of whether your employer does. You are worth it!

ESSAY 7: FIVE CRITICAL CONCEPTS FOR SUCCESSFUL IT CAREERS

Watch the companion video at https://youtu.be/ytTdFzgxwdA

As IT pros, we understand the technology we work with, but successful careers in IT involve much more than the technical aspects of knowing how to code, set up a server, or configure a router. Here are five concepts that IT pros need to understand if they want to achieve success in their careers.

Career Concept #1: Our Jobs Are Not About Technology; They Are About Helping Other People Do Their Jobs

Sure, we work in technology, and our jobs require a deep understanding of the technologies with which we work. Still, if we are not solving human problems in the workplace, what is the point of what we do? We may be masters of configuring access control lists or building apps, but if such tasks don't serve people, there is no point to them. I love working with various aspects of technology, sometimes even to the point of distraction. Ultimately, however, the work that I perform must serve people.

Career Concept #2: We Must Stay Up to Date on Technology and Culture

Even though our careers are built on serving people, technology is the main tool we use to provide that service. Technology advances at a mind boggling and exponentially increasing pace. Bill Gates even referred to doing "business at the speed of thought."

The in-depth understanding we gain today will be obsolete soon. Some of what we know today may be useful as a foundation for tomorrow's required knowledge, but much of today's knowledge will be useless in tomorrow's world. Consider how little demand there is for a Windows 95 expert today! In our field, there's no room for anyone mired in yesterday's technology, culture, or behaviors. The world is changing. Sure, you can fight it, but you can't stop it. Get used to it.

Career Concept #3: There's a Difference Between Being Honest and Being Rude

Authenticity has become a popular business buzzword recently. Authenticity, or candor, allows us to make informed decisions, helps us keep from repeating our mistakes, and challenges our preconceived notions about how things work. Sometimes, however, those of us who work in technology forget that we are working with human beings, and we forget that authenticity must be combined with sensitivity. Argumentative people are off-putting and rude. They may win a few battles, but they'll lose the war as they lose the support of their colleagues. Certainly it is important to stand up for ourselves lest we risk losing the respect of our colleagues, bosses, and clients. But you need not put another person down to stand up for yourself. Choose your words carefully. To quote author Meryl Runion, "say what you mean, mean what you say, and don't be mean when you say it" (Runion 2010).

Career Concept #4: When People Like You, They'll Go to Bat for You

Perhaps you've heard people say that they don't care whether they are liked by other people so long as they are respected. Although respect is certainly important, if people like you, they'll stand up for you and your ideas even when your back is turned. In my training seminars, we often talk about whether we are creating advocates or detractors behind our backs. When people both respect and like you, they'll be more likely to be an advocate for you during hall conversations, in break rooms, and around the water cooler. Being likable doesn't necessarily mean that you are gregarious and outgoing. It also doesn't mean that you agree with everything other people say or believe. It could simply mean that people find you pleasant and easy to be around. The use of basic manners can go a long way toward helping people come over to your side. Be polite.

Career Concept #5: Patience Is a Virtue

The saying is as true as it is old: good things come to those who are willing to wait. Sometimes organizations move very slowly. If you work in government, for example, things can seem as if they are moving at a snail's pace. Change can happen, however, given enough time. People and organizations, like morning traffic, often move much more slowly than we'd like. But be patient and persistent, and your career will benefit.

Our jobs, in information systems and technology, are not about technology. Our jobs are about helping our end users, our customers, work more productively, effectively, and creatively. Our jobs are about crafting creative technical solutions to perplexing human problems in the workplace.

EPILOGUE

You are part of something very big and very important.

Today, there is a global awakening taking place, the likes of which we haven't seen since the Renaissance.

It started in 1959 when Paul Baran conceived the idea of packet switching networks. His idea was to create a fault-tolerant communications network which could withstand a Soviet Union first nuclear strike.

Over the next 10 years, people conducted research which led to the launch in 1969 of the ARPANET, the predecessor of today's global Internet. The goal of the ARPANET was to facilitate communication and collaboration among researchers.

Many people were and are involved in the development of the Internet. Some of the best known names include Vinton Cerf and Robert Kahn who created the TCP/IP protocols, Sir Tim Berners-Lee who created the World Wide Web, and Marc Andreesen who, with Eric Bina, created the first graphical point and click browser.

There are, of course, many other people who have contributed and continue to contribute to the amazing global communications and collaboration project known as the Internet. (You can learn more about the birth and growth of the Internet and the people involved by searching on "history of the Internet".)

Today, people from across the globe can quickly share information and ideas. The Internet provides the opportunity for people in one part of the world to learn about people in another part of the world, to study art, science, or philosophy, to start businesses, to video chat with grandparents, and yes, to watch funny animal videos. Crowdsourcing makes it possible for an inventor to get funding for an invention that might change the world and for musicians and artists to get funding for new works that could make our world a better or more beautiful place. The Internet allows authors to connect directly with fans. New ideas can quickly spread worldwide.

This amazing phenomenon is possible thanks to the geeks and nerds of the world, people like you and me who have a fascination and knack for technology. Today's data networks provide the foundational fabric that underlies all communication and which makes possible the sharing of ideas and information. It makes possible global collaboration. Whether you are a coder writing apps, a network manager in a small business, a database manager, a help desk technician, an enterprise solutions architect, or any other person involved in information systems and technology, your job is very important. Your skills are critical to the success of the organization you support. It is your technical knowledge that allows the other people in your organization to do their jobs more productively, effectively, and creatively. Never question the value of what you do.

You are extremely important to both your organization and to the world.

I'm honored to be a small part of the information systems and technology field. I wish you tremendous success and happiness in your life.

REFERENCES

Baren-Cohen, S. 2011. *The Science of Evil: On Empathy and the Origins of Cruelty.* New York: Basic Books.

Covey, S. R. (1989) 2004. *The 7 Habits of Highly Effective People.* New York: Free Press.

Cuddy, A. 2015. *Presence.* New York: Little, Brown, and Company.

Frankl, V. E. (1946, 1959, 1962) 1984. *Man's Search for Meaning.* New York: Pocket Books.

Goleman, D. D. 1995. *Emotional Intelligence: Why It Can Matter More Than IQ.* New York: Bantam Dell.

Hallowell, E. 1999. "The Human Moment at Work." *Harvard Business Review* (January): 58–66. https://hbr.org/1999/01/the-human-moment-at-work.

Harris, S. 2013. *Lying.* Vancouver, BC: Four Elephants Press.

Kida, T. E. 2006. *Don't Believe Everything You Think: The 6 Basic Mistakes We Make in Thinking.* Amherst, NY: Prometheus Books.

Lally, P. v. 2010. "How are habits formed? Modelling habit formation in the real world." *European Journal of Social Psychology,* 998–1009.

Roth, B. 2015. *The Achievement Habit: Stop Wishing, Start Doing, and Take Command of Your Life.* New York: HarperCollins Publishers.

Runion, M. 2010. *Power Phrases: The Perfect Words to Say It Right and Get the Results You Want.* New York: Morgan James Publishing.

ABOUT THE AUTHOR

Don R. Crawley is a lifelong geek. He holds multiple technical certifications and has written eight books for IT pros on topics ranging from Cisco firewalls and Linux servers to compassionate customer service. He lives with Janet, his wife, in Seattle, Washington, where he enjoys watching the ships on Puget Sound and laughing with his family. In his spare time, he plays the pipe organ.

Learn more about Don at www.doncrawley.com. Follow him on Twitter: @DonCrawley, Facebook: www.fb.com/DonRCrawley, and LinkedIn: www.linkedin.com/in/doncrawley.

Book Don for your next meeting, conference, or convention: www.doncrawley.com/info or call him at (206) 988-5858. Watch his demo video at www.doncrawley.com/demoreel.

THE COMPASSIONATE GEEK®

Customer Service Skills for Tech People

PROGRAMS

- *Keynote: How to be a Compassionate Geek (20 to 90 minutes)*
- *Training: Customer Service, Compassion, and Computers: Making Them Work Together to Enhance Customer Relationships (3 to 12 hours)*

www.doncrawley.com/presentations

WHAT CLIENTS HAVE TO SAY:

"Don was very approachable and helpful ... He knew the material well and seemed to personally be interested and into it."

— Facebook, Navid Mansourian

"His thought-provoking testimonies, suggestions and advice given during his presentation were eye opening, even though I thought going in that I knew how to show compassion to my 'customers' when providing technology support. I would highly recommend Don."

— DISC Conference, Roni Argetsinger

www.doncrawley.com/customer-reviews

HOW TO BE A COMPASSIONATE GEEK

Success strategies for you and your IT staff

- Improve collaboration and productivity
- Implement the five principles of IT customer service
- Develop emotional intelligence skills
- Learn solid skills for dealing with difficult customers
- Build excellent listening skills
- Uncover ways to show you care
- Master communication through email and other text-based communication tools
- Learn how to say "no" without alienating your end user
- Learn how to manage your stress

www.doncrawley.com/presentations

Request information online at www.doncrawley.com/info

CONTACT DON CRAWLEY, CSP • PROFESSIONAL SPEAKER

Call (206) 988-5858 • Email: don@doncrawley.com
P.O. Box 48094, Seattle, WA 98148

CRAWLEY
INTERNATIONAL, INC.

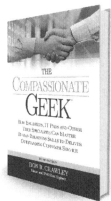

Made in the USA
Middletown, DE
23 October 2017